In Remembrance of a
Special Dog

A KEEPSAKE MEMORIAL

In Remembrance of a
Special Dog

A Collection of
Inspirational Writings

Compiled and edited by
RICHARD F. X. O'CONNOR

RENAISSANCE BOOKS
Los Angeles

The editor acknowledges with gratitude permission to include the following: "Request From Rainbow Bridge" by Constance Jenkins; excerpts from "The Best Cat Book Ever" by Cleveland Amory, text copyright © 1993 by Cleveland Amory, reprinted with the permission of Little, Brown and Company; excerpt from "All Creatures Great And Small," by James Herriot, copyright © by James Herriot, Michael Joseph Publishers and copyright © 1972 by James Herriot, reprinted with the permission of St. Martin's Press; "Godspeed" by Marianne Hudz, copyright © 1995 by Marianne Hudz, reprinted with the permission of the author; "Jet" by Louise Andrae-Ramsey, copyright © 1997, reprinted with the permission of the author.

Due diligence has been exercised in attempting to locate all owners of material herein. Permissions have not been obtained from anonymous authors or from those authors not found by publisher despite its due diligence as of the date of publication. The editor would be grateful to receive any updated information.

Special thanks to interns Ryan P. Romines and Michael Mahin who assisted in the collection of the verse in this book.

97   98   99   00   10   9   8   7   6   5   4   3   2   1

Library of Congress Cataloging-in-Publication Data:

In remembrance of a special dog: a collection of inspirational writings/compiled and edited by Richard F. X. O'Connor.
     p.   cm.
   ISBN 1-58063-005-7 (hc: alk. paper)
   1. Dogs—Quotations, maxims, etc. I. O'Connor, Richard F. X.
PN6084.D64I56   1998
636.7—dc21   97-44435
                                                   CIP

PRINTED IN MEXICO

For Gypsy
who taught us
not to stop short

In loving memory of
Schultzy and Snickers

*Place
Photo
Here*

Inscription

for

_____

In Loving
Remembrance of

_____

from

_____

Foreword

From the very earliest days of my ministry as a newly ordained pastor, I was confronted with grief over the loss of loved ones. On such occasions, the Scriptures always held out comfort, hope, and consolation.

Imagine my surprise and challenge when a five-year-old parishioner requested that I conduct the funeral of her beloved parakeet. To this young girl the spiritual well-being of her animal friend was of paramount importance. In recent months I was invited back to that small town to celebrate the fortieth birthday of that young lady and was quite moved to find that the death, grief, and healing of that experience was indelibly fixed in her mind as well as in mine.

Throughout my days of active pastoral ministry, spanning more than thirty-five years, and to the time of my retirement from Norview Baptist Church in Norfolk, Virginia, time after time it was my solemn duty and privilege to offer comfort to those who were grieving the loss of a cat, dog, or other special pet friend. And yes, I conducted other pet funerals invoking divine healing of broken hearts.

Grief is so painfully real, regardless of its origin. The love of, and attachment to, an animal friend can equal that of human relationships. Likewise, the loss of an animal can be just as devastating. May this gift evoke equal understanding, compassion and hope to all in need.

—*Reverend Joel L. Morgan*
Richmond, Virginia, 1997

B uy a pup
   and your money will buy
   Love unflinching
   that cannot lie.

Rudyard Kipling

Rainbow Bridge

Just this side of heaven is a place called Rainbow Bridge. When an animal dies that has been especially close to someone here, that pet goes to Rainbow Bridge.

There are meadows and hills for all of our special friends so they can run and play together. There is plenty of food, water and sunshine, and our friends are warm and comfortable.

All the animals who had been ill and old are restored to health and vigor; those who were hurt or maimed are made whole and strong again, just as we remember them in our dreams of days and times gone by.

The animals are happy and content, except for one small thing: they miss someone very special to them, who had to be left behind. They run and play together, but the day comes when one suddenly stops and looks into the distance. His bright eyes are intent; his eager body quivers. Suddenly he begins to run from the group, flying over the green grass, his legs carrying him faster and faster.

You have been spotted, and when you and your special friend finally meet, you cling together in joyous reunion, never to be parted again. The happy kisses rain upon your face; your hands again caress the beloved head, and you look once more into the trusting eyes of your pet, so long gone from your life but never absent from your heart.

Then you cross Rainbow Bridge together....

Anonymous
FROM THE INTERNET

The best friend a man has in this world may turn against him and become his enemy. The money that a man has he may lose.

The one absolutely unselfish friend that man can have in this selfish world, the one that never deserts him, the one that never moves ungrateful or treacherous, is his dog. He will kiss the hand that has no food to offer. When all other friends desert, he remains.

If fortune drives the master forth an outcast in the world, friendless and homeless, the faithful dog asks no higher privilege than that of accompanying him to guard against danger, to fight his enemies, and when the last scene of all comes, and death takes the master in its embrace and his body is laid away in the cold ground, no matter if all other friends pursue their way, there by his graveside will the noble dog be found, his head between his paws, his eyes sad but open on alert watchfulness, faithful and true even to death.

George G. Vest

JET

My grandfather believed every child should have a dog. "A dog," he said, "could teach a child many things—about relationships, responsibility, love and respect." So Jet came into our lives, a black ball of fur. Jet protected my brother and me through all the joys and pains of childhood, into teen years.

Ever loyal and faithful, he guarded our family against all threats that crossed his ken. Never mean-spirited, Jet was always gentle with children. And I believed him smart, because I could tell him anything and he always listened, never giving me away. It broke my heart when his time came. Yet still I think of Jet, my loving animal.

My grandfather was right. Every child should have a dog ... a dog can teach a child many things.

Anne-Louise Andrae

There is sorrow enough in the natural way
From men and women to fill our day,
And when we are certain of sorrow in store
Why do we always arrange for more?
Brothers and Sisters, I bid you beware
Of giving your heart to a dog, to tear.

Rudyard Kipling

The more I see of men,
the more I admire dogs.

Madame Roland

Let's spend while we may,
Each dog hath his day.

J. P. Collier
ROXBURGHE BALLADS

All knowledge,
the totality of all questions and answers,
is contained in the dog.

Franz Kafka

Request from Rainbow Bridge

Weep not for me though I am gone
Into that gentle night.
Grieve if you will, but not for long
Upon my soul's sweet flight.
I am at peace, my soul's at rest
There is no need for tears.
There is no pain, I suffer not,
The fear now all is gone.
Put now these things out of your thoughts,
In your memory I live on.
Remember not my fight for breath
Remember not the strife
Please do not dwell upon my death,
But celebrate my life.

Constance Jenkins

I am called a dog
because I fawn on those who give anything,
I yelp at those who refuse,
and I set my teeth in rascals.

Diogenes

If you pick up a starving dog
and make him prosperous,
he will not bite you.
This is the principal difference
between a dog and a man.

Mark Twain

Near this spot are deposited the remains
of one who possessed Beauty without Vanity,
Strength without Insolence,
Courage without Ferocity,
and all the Virtues of Man without Vices.
This Praise,
which would be unmeaning Flattery
if inscribed over human ashes,
is but a just tribute
to the Memory of Boatswain, a Dog.

Lord Byron

Most high and holy,
most powerful Lord....

To Thee and Thy creatures
we proffer our praise
Who brings us the beauty
and joy of our days....

They shall merit Thy crown.

St. Francis of Assisi

Godspeed

Good-bye, Magic.
Don't be afraid.
There's no more pain for you now, old girl.
No leashes.
No "bad dog."
No fences.
Look—
There's green, green grass
and laughing children
a cat to chase
shady trees to lie down by
and a master who's always glad to see you.
You're going home now.
I wish you safe passage and plenty of bones.
I wish you a sturdy pull-ring
a high-bouncing ball
and a strong, forever-young boy to play with.
Some day I'll find you.

Marianne Hudz

I am his Highness' dog at Kew;
Pray tell me, sir, whose dog are you?

Alexander Pope

He cannot be a gentleman
which loveth not a dog.

John Northbrooke

He's dead. Oh! lay him gently in the ground!
And may his tomb be by this verse renowned:
Here Shock, the pride of all his kind, is laid,
Who fawned like man but ne'er like man betrayed.

John Gay

The reason a dog has so many friends
is that he wags his tail instead of his tongue.

Anonymous

Recollect that the Almighty,
who gave the dog to be companion
of our pleasures and our toils,
hath invested him
with a nature noble
and incapable of deceit.

Sir Walter Scott

The old dog barks backward without getting up.
I can remember when he was a pup.

Robert Frost

Do not stand at my grave and weep,
I am not there, I do not sleep.
I am a thousand winds that blow;
I am the diamond glints on snow.
I am the sunlight on ripened grain;
I am the gentle autumn's rain.
When you awaken in the morning's hush,
I am the sweet uplifting rush
Of quiet birds in circled flight
I am the first star that shines at night.
Do not stand at my grave and cry,
I am not there. I did not die.

Anonymous

The poor dog,
in life the firmest friend.
The first to welcome,
foremost to defend.

Lord Byron

Love me, love my dog.

LATIN PROVERB

There are three faithful friends
— an old wife,
an old dog,
and ready money.

Benjamin Franklin

I think God will have prepared everything for our perfect happiness (in Heaven). If it takes my dog being there, I believe he'll be there.

Reverend Billy Graham

...admitted to that equal sky,
His faithful dog shall bear him company.

Alexander Pope

When a puppy takes fifty catnaps
in the course of a day,
he cannot always be expected
to sleep the night through.
It is too much to ask.

Albert Payson Terhune

 I realize something I did not realize then—how lucky I was compared to so many others who have to face the loss of their animal without other people around them. I, at least, was surrounded by animal people.

And I think they've got to let the person know that it's O.K., that grief for a pet *is* acceptable, it *is* normal.

Unlike some people who have experienced the loss of an animal, I did not believe, even for a moment, that I would never get another. I did know full well that there were just too many animals out there in need of homes for me to take what I have always regarded as the self-indulgent road of saying the heartbreak of the loss of an animal was too much ever to want to go through with it again. To me, such an admission brought up the far more powerful admission that all the wonderful times you had with your animal were not worth the unhappiness at the end.

Cleveland Amory

A dog can express more
with his tail in minutes
than his owner can express
with his tongue in hours.

Anonymous

Dog. A kind of additional
or subsidiary Deity designed
to catch the overflow and surplus
of the world's worship.

Ambrose Bierce

Therefore to this dog will I,
tenderly, not scornfully,
Render praise and favor:
With my hand upon his head,
Is my benediction said
Therefore and forever.

Elizabeth Barrett Browning

To mark a friend's remains
these stones arise;
I never knew but one—
and here he lies.

Lord Byron

The great pleasure of a dog
is that you may make a fool of yourself with him
and not only will he not scold you,
but he will make a fool of himself too.

Samuel Butler

His friends he loved. His direst earthly foes—
Cats—I believe he did not but feign to hate.
My hand will miss the insinuated nose,
Mine eyes the tail that wagg'd contempt at Fate.

Sir William Watson

M ajor
Born a dog
Died a gentleman

Epitaph

O ur German forefathers had a very kind religion.
They believed that, after death,
they would meet again all the good dogs
that had been their companions in life.

Otto Von Bismarck

Every boy should have two things:
a dog
and a mother willing to let him have one.

Anonymous

I had rather be a dog,
and bay the moon,
than such a Roman.

Brutus to Cassius
IN WILLIAM SHAKESPEARE'S
JULIUS CAESAR

 Anyone who has had to go through an animal's death knows what it is like to come upon a favorite toy, a favorite ball... or indeed a favorite anything. Even a dish can do it.

But even coming across one of your animal's things is not by all means all of what you must go through. At such a time, even a look at your animal's favorite places will be too much for you, if you are anything like me, you will not only see and hear your animal before you go to sleep—if indeed you can sleep—you will even feel his paws padding on your bed and then, after that, you will dream about him.

Now, of course, there was nothing.... The whole apartment had, for me, become an empty nothingness. It was not just that Polar Bear was not there—it was the awful, overpowering weight of knowing he was never ever going to be there again.

Cleveland Amory

Ed. note: The author's comforting prose warranted inclusion in this collection, even though Polar Bear was a cat.

Dogs are not only a product
of their own temperament,
but of their owner's as well.
You never really train a dog,
so much as train the owner.

Anonymous

On the green banks of Shannon, when
    Sheelah was nigh,
No blithe Irish lad was so happy as I;
No harp like my own could so cheerily
    play,
And wherever I went was my poor dog Tray.

Thomas Campbell

One reason a dog is such a comfort
when you're downcast
is that he doesn't ask to know why.

Anonymous

The more I see of the representatives
of the people, the more I admire my dogs.

Alphonse De Lamartine

When a dog bites a man, that
is not news,
because it happens so often.
But if a man bites a dog,
that is news.

John B. Bogart
City Editor of the New York Sun

They say a reasonable number of
fleas is good fer a dog
—keeps him from broodin' over bein' a dog.

Edward Noyes Westcott

Never another pet for me!
Let your place all vacant be;
Better blackness day by day
Than companion torn away.
Better bid his memory fade,
Better blot each mark he made,
Selfishly escape distress
By contrived forgetfulness,
Than preserve his prints to make
Every morn and eve an ache.

Housemate, I can think you still
Bounding to the window-sill,
Over which I vaguely see
Your small mound beneath the tree,
Showing in the autumn shade
That you moulder where you played.

Thomas Hardy

The gingham dog went "Bow-wow-wow!"
And the calico cat replied "Mee-ow!"
The air was littered, an hour or so,
With bits of gingham and calico.

Eugene Field

 Children and dogs
are as necessary
to the welfare of the country
as Wall Street and the railroads.

Harry S. Truman

I went back and sat down by the bed. Miss Stubbs looked out the window for a few minutes, then turned to me. "You know, Mr. Herriot," she said casually. "It will be my turn next. I have only one fear." Her expression changed with startling suddenness as if a mask had dropped. A kind of terror flickered in her eyes and she quickly grasped my hand.

"It's my dogs and cats, Mr. Herriot. I'm afraid I might never see them when I'm gone and it worries me so. You see, I know I'll be reunited with my parents and my brothers but… "

"Well, why not with your animals?"

"That's just it." She rocked her head on the pillow and for the first time I saw tears on her cheeks. "They say animals have no souls."

"Miss Stubbs, I'm afraid I'm a bit foggy on all this," I said. "But I'm absolutely certain of one thing. Wherever you are going, they are going too."

She stared at me but her face was calm again. "Thank you, Mr. Herriot, I know you are being honest with me. That's what you really believe, isn't it?"

"I do believe it," I said. "With all my heart I believe it."

James Herriot

His puppyhood was a period
of foolish rebellion.
He was always worsted,
but he fought back
because it was his nature
to fight back.
And he was unconquerable.

Jack London

My little dog:
a heart-beat at my feet.

Edith Wharton

Histories are more full of examples
of the fidelity of dogs
than of friends.

Alexander Pope

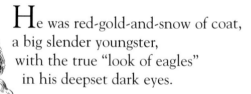

He was red-gold-and-snow of coat,
a big slender youngster,
with the true "look of eagles"
in his deepset dark eyes.

Albert Payson Terhune

F. D. R. and the Rescue of Fala

Political opponents of F. D. R. accused the President of wasting money to send a United States warship to rescue his dog, Fala, allegedly stranded on an island.

Said the President, "These Republican leaders have not been content with attacks on me, or my wife, or on my sons. No, not content with that, they now include my little dog, Fala. Well, of course, I don't resent attacks… but Fala does resent them. His Scotch soul was furious. He has not been the same dog since."

Place
Photo
Here

There remains, to those who have lost an animal, two large questions. The first of these involves whether or not to bury your animal. I have always believed that the best place to bury your animal is in your heart. I fully believe that.

The second large question—do animals go to heaven? I do believe that we and our animals will meet again. If we do not, and where we go is supposed to be heaven, it will not be heaven to me and it will not be where I wish to go.

Cleveland Amory

Place
Photo
Here

THE FIVE STAGES OF GRIEF

DENIAL

•

BARGAINING

•

ANGER

•

GRIEF

•

RESOLUTION

Pet Loss Help Lines

Chicago Veterinary
Medical Association/Delta Society
Pet Loss Help Line
(708) 603-3994

University of Florida at Gainesville
Pet Loss Hotline
(904) 338-2032

University of California at Davis
Pet Loss Help Line
(916) 752-4200

The Delta Society
(800) 869-6898